AF270649

How Do I Research Well?

Sarah Eason and
Louise Spilsbury

Please visit our website, www.cheritonchildrensbooks.com to see more of our high-quality books.

First Edition

Published in 2022 by **Cheriton Children's Books**
PO Box 7258, Bridgnorth WV16 9ET, UK

Authors: Sarah Eason and Louise Spilsbury
Designer: Paul Myerscough
Editor: Jennifer Sanderson
Picture Researcher: Rachel Blount
Proofreader: Wendy Scavuzzo

Picture credits: Cover: Shutterstock/Julia Kuznetsova. Inside: p1: Shutterstock/myboys.me; p4: Shutterstock/O_Lypa; p5: Shutterstock/LightField Studios; p6: Shutterstock/stockphoto-graf; p7: Shutterstock/insta_photos; p8: Shutterstock/Susan Leggett; p9: Shutterstock/TommyStockProject; p10: Shutterstock/Blackday; p11: Shutterstock/Roman Samborskyi; p12: Shutterstock/Iakov Filimonov; p13: Shutterstock/Fizkes; p14: Shutterstock/Vaclav Sebek; p15: Shutterstock/Prostock-studio; p16: Shutterstock/myboys.me; p17: Shutterstock/Evan Lorne; p18: Shutterstock/Andrey Armyagov; p19: Shutterstock/Syda Productions; p20: Shutterstock/Tatyana Soares; p21: Shutterstock/BAZA Production; p22: Shutterstock/Odua Images; p23: Shutterstock/Africa Studio; p24: Shutterstock/Roman Samborskyi; p25: Shutterstock/Md Rasel 09; p26: Shutterstock/Syda Productions; p27: Shutterstock/Ihor Bulyhin; p28: Shutterstock/Syda Productions; p29: Shutterstock/Sunny studio.

Printed in the United States of America

Contents

Help! How Do I Research?

#Help! Your class has been given a **research** project —and your teacher says you have to hand it in next week. #Research—AreYouForReal?! But before you freak out, take a breath. Research is not nearly as scary as it sounds. In fact, anyone can learn how to research. And once you know how to do it well, it can be really fun, too. Feeling research-ready? Then let's get started…

You'll be amazed by how research helps you create really great schoolwork.

Research—What's So Great?

Good research helps you create great projects. By reading this book and discovering better research skills, you will learn to:

- Plan a research project.
- Carry out a research project.
- Use **informational** books, **encyclopedias**, and other useful library books.
- Improve the way you use the Internet for research.
- Read through **sources** quickly to find the information that you need.
- Discover the best way to take notes and organize them.

But, research isn't just for school. It's a really important life skill, too. Being able to find and use information helps you make choices. Research skills help you find information in different places. They help you reach conclusions and **communicate** well, too.

#Help!

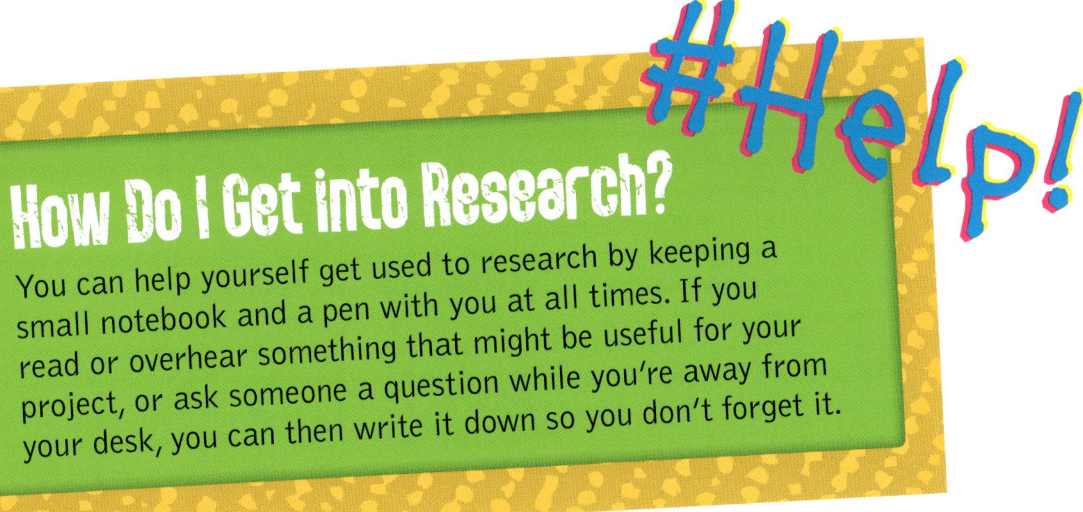

How Do I Get into Research?

You can help yourself get used to research by keeping a small notebook and a pen with you at all times. If you read or overhear something that might be useful for your project, or ask someone a question while you're away from your desk, you can then write it down so you don't forget it.

Find Out to Figure It Out

Have you ever bought something and then later wished that you hadn't? Maybe if you had done a little research first, you may have made a better choice. When people are researching an important purchase, they don't use just one source of information to discover what they need to know. They may ask friends and look on the Internet. They read **reports** in newspapers, magazines, and sales catalogs. They check different **reliable** sources. They make notes so that they can make a decision based on all of the information they find. That's what you need to do in preparation for reports and projects. You need to research by gathering information from a wide variety of reliable sources. Then you can come to a conclusion and figure out a final plan.

Don't let research projects spook you! Once you have learned to research, you can teach your friends how to do it, too.

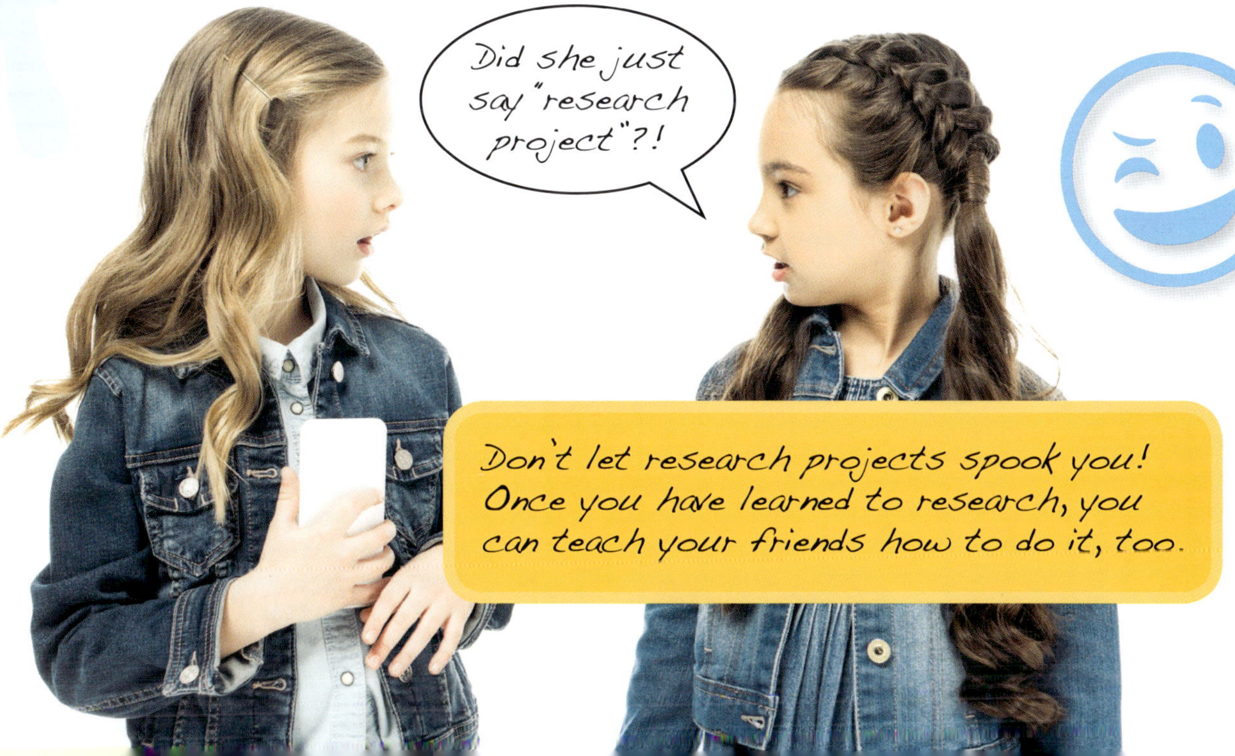

Chapter One

Help! How Do I Start Researching?

#Don'tKnowWhereToStart! If you feel freaked out about beginning your research project, don't worry. The first step is easy—you just need to be clear about what information you're going to look for before you start. If you are researching a school project, you'll usually be given a subject to work on. The most important thing is to be sure you understand what type of project you are going to work on. That way, you will research the correct information.

What Do I Need?

Different types of projects require different types of information. Check that you understand what you're being asked to do before you begin researching. Then you can collect the right material from the start.

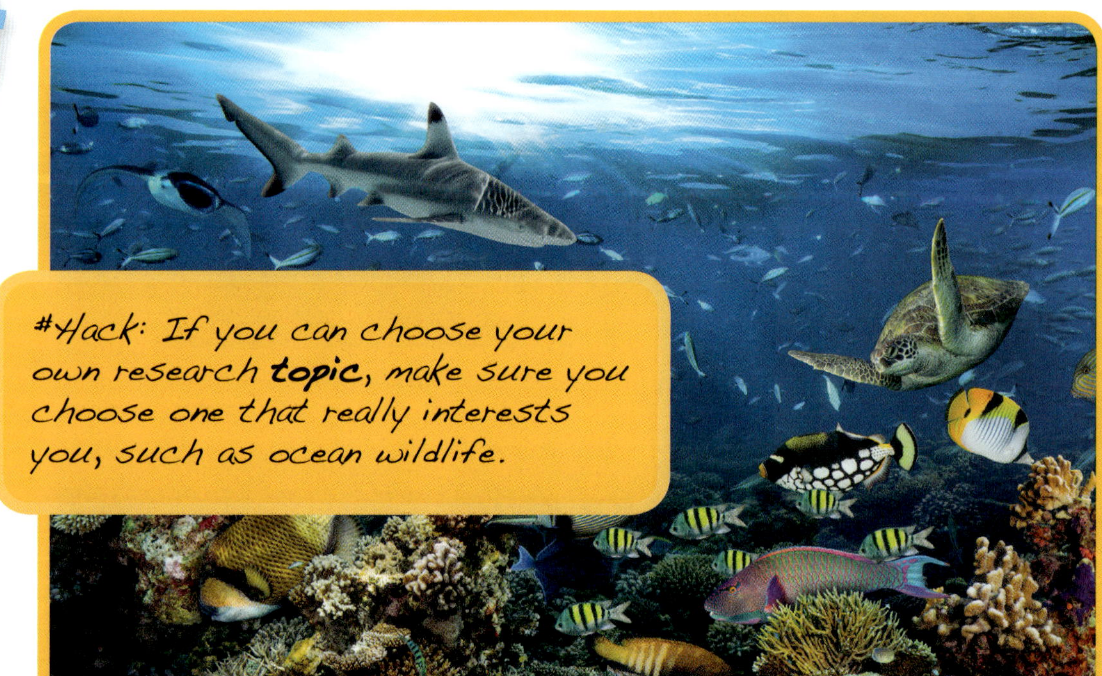

- Informational essays require information from books, **journals**, and other sources.
- Posters require drawings and photographs.
- Reports about an event in the past or an **opinion** piece may benefit from **quotes**. They help explain events firsthand.
- PowerPoint presentations require images and possibly videos clips.
- A local history project requires interviews with family, friends, or other local people.

Look for the Clues

With every research project, clues about what to look for are in the description. These are words that tell you important parts of the project. Let's take a look at key words to watch for.

- *Compare and contrast.* This means you should describe similarities and differences among things.
- *Describe or outline.* This means you should explain the main facts about the subject in question.
- *Discuss.* This means you should give the pros and cons of opposite sides of an argument.
- *Justify or explain.* This means you should say how and why something happens, using examples and **evidence**.
- *Demonstrate or show.* This means you should give examples to prove something.

It helps to make note of all the information you will require for your research project before you start researching.

How Do I Make It Easier?

Sometimes you may be given a broad topic title for a research project, such as "**Ecosystems.**" This is a large, complicated topic, so it might help to concentrate on one feature of it. Instead of writing about "Ecosystems," you could look at "**Food Chains** in Ecosystems."

Nada, zilch, nothing?! Well, I bet you know more than you think you know! When you are given a new research topic, you'll probably already know a little about it. For example, if your teacher gives you a history research project, the chances are you will have worked on the topic in class a little already. That's why, before you start working on your project, you need to find what you already know and do some background reading to find out even more. But how do you check what you already know? You brainstorm!

Get Inside Your Head

Brainstorming helps you discover what you already know about a topic. To brainstorm, try the following:

- Sit down with a pen or a computer. Then, write whatever comes into your head about your topic, even if you think it's wrong.

You Can Hack It!

Can you think of situations in which brainstorming could help you find out what you already know about something? For example, how might brainstorming what you know about a rival sports team help you before you play against them?

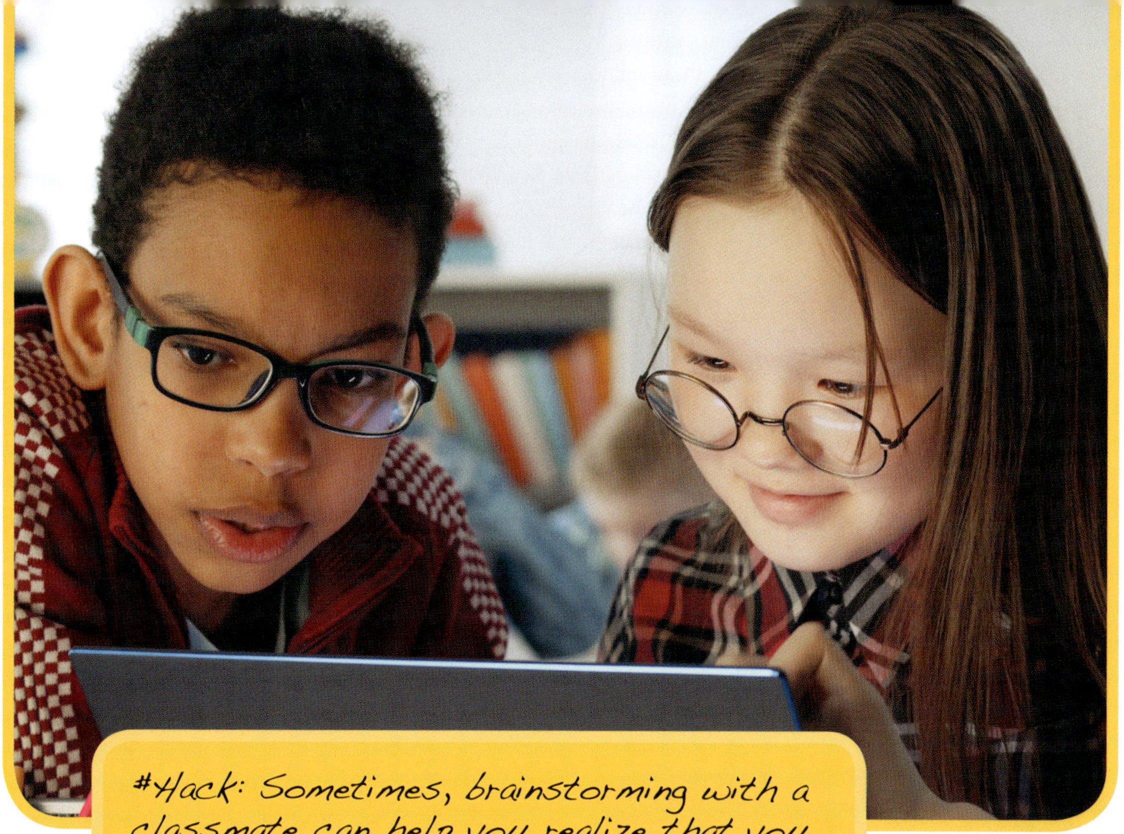

#Hack: Sometimes, brainstorming with a classmate can help you realize that you know a lot more than you might think.

- Write down as many ideas as you can. Keep writing for around three to five minutes.
- Don't worry about spelling, **grammar**, or neat writing as you write down your ideas.

When you read through what you've written down, you may have some useful ideas that can be developed for your research project.

Enter the Encyclopedia!

It's a good idea to gather some background information about your topic before you begin your research. An encyclopedia is a great place to find background information. Encyclopedias have short entries that give you a useful **overview** of most subjects. They are usually arranged alphabetically, and have guide words at the top of every page to help you find the right entry. You can use that information to build up a list of key words to help with your research. For example, if an encyclopedia tells you that snakes are **reptiles**, you can research the word "reptile" as well as "snake."

Why Should I Use Sources?

Ok, so you're ready to start researching, but where do you start looking? Well, have you ever heard the saying, "Go to the source?" That means go to the place where the information first came from. To carry out research well, you will need to use more than one source. But which different sources should you look at? And what are the differences between them? Read on, research rookie!

This Mayan carving is an example of a primary source. You might use it in a research project about the Maya.

You Heard It Here First!

Sources used for research are usually divided into two groups, primary sources and secondary sources. Primary sources are **original**, firsthand accounts or evidence about a person, a place, an object, or an event. The account might be from someone who experienced the event. It might be from a person who knew the person you wish to write about. Primary sources are records of something that happened, or was said or thought about at one point in time. Examples of primary sources include letters, photographs, and diaries. They also include videos, interviews, **autobiographies**, and speeches.

Next Up

Secondary sources are secondhand accounts. They are written or created by people some time after an event. They explain, comment on, or draw conclusions from primary sources.

Examples of secondary sources include textbooks, history books, and encyclopedias. Newspaper and magazine **articles** can be primary or secondary sources. If the article was written when something happened or just afterward, it is a primary source. If a reporter writes about an event in the past, using information written by someone else, it is a secondary source.

Source It Yourself

One way to find primary information is to source it yourself. For a topic about a local issue, you could talk to people in your community. You could carry out interviews and record the answers. You could also **conduct** a **survey**, with a list of questions and spaces for answers.

What Do I Trust?

Secondary sources are easier to find than many primary sources. However, it is important to use reliable secondary sources—ones that you can trust. Here is how to discover if a secondary source is reliable:

- Find out who wrote the secondary source—are they trustworthy?
- Discover if the author used evidence to support their ideas.
- Check that the author has an obvious opinion about the topic.

You might use a magazine article as a secondary source. Your mom or dad might read a newspaper to find information. That is also a secondary source.

Think books are boring? Think again! Books are a great place to start your research. That is because they have been researched and checked by professional writers and **publishers**. They have also been **edited**. If you choose the right books, they can provide reliable and interesting information. But, how do you go about choosing which books to read?

Full of Facts

Reference books include dictionaries, **atlases**, and encyclopedias. Informational books usually **focus** on one topic or subject, such as animals, volcanoes, or world religions. Reference books are a great way to find reliable information about your topic. One of the advantages of reference books is that they are carefully chosen by librarians. Librarians are experts at choosing good quality, reliable books. They have also probably found **resources** about your topic for other students before.

> #Hack: Learn to love the library! It's a great place to fact-find.

How Do I Use the Library? #Help!

Libraries are great—just ask your school librarian! A library can have hundreds or even thousands of books. But what's the best way to find the books you need?

- Browse the shelves. Books are usually divided into subjects, such as sports and history. Use the divisions to help you find your topics.
- Use the library catalog. This is usually a computer that is easy to use. You can search for the name of the book, the author, or the subject you need.
- Ask library staff to help you find information. Most librarians will go out of their way to help you.

Books are trustworthy sources of information because writers carefully research and check their facts.

How Do I Use Books?

OK, so you made it to the library. You found a stack of books. And now—you just have to read them, cover to cover! #SayWhat?! Just kidding! The good news is you don't have to. Books have features such as **indexes** and chapters to help you quickly find the information you need. Phew, that's a load off…!

It's All About the Content

Informational and reference books usually begin with a table of contents. This is a list of the parts of the book, listed in the order in which they appear. The table helps you find your way around the text inside. It usually includes the titles of the chapters or sections in the book, and tells you which page they start on. Let's say you pick up a book about animals of the world, but your project is about tigers. You should be able to use the contents list to go straight to the **relevant** section, without reading any of the other pages.

#Help!

How Do I Find the Pictures?

Indexes can also help you to find illustrations, photographs, maps, or diagrams. In some indexes, you will see page numbers in boldface, such as **112** or **16**. That means there will be an illustration about the subject on that page.

"I" Is for Index

An index is another useful tool for quickly finding your way around a book. You'll usually find the index at the back of informational and reference books. It is a list of all the important parts and topics of the book, and is arranged in alphabetical order. If an animal book doesn't have a separate chapter about tigers, simply go to the index. Look in the list of entries under the letter "T" to find the pages where tigers are mentioned.

Chapter Two

Help! How Do I Search the Internet?

#NeedToGetOnTheNet! The Internet is another great place to carry out your research. However, there is an unbelievably huge amount information on the World Wide Web. There are well over 150 million websites, and some are made up of hundreds of thousands of web pages! The Internet is an online library of endless primary and secondary sources. So where do you start?

Seek It Out

You can use search engines such as Yahoo!, Bing, or Google to find out about a subject. To use a search engine, type the topic you are searching for into the search box. Then, click on "search." You will get better results if you type more than one word into the search box. For example, if you want information about penguins, don't just type in "birds." Try to be more specific.

Once you know how to use them well, search engines can do a lot of the hard research work for you.

#Help!

How Do I Find Information?

Try these suggestions to improve your Internet searches:

- Avoid writing complete sentences when you are searching. Use key words instead, such as writing "wolves," rather than "Where can I find information about wolves?"
- Check your spelling. Most search engines will search for exactly what you have typed in.
- Use quotation marks. If you're looking for a short phrase, or two to four words that go together, put them in quotation marks, such as "gray wolf."
- You can search for one word and exclude another by using a minus sign. For example, to search for tigers, but not Siberian tigers, you would type "tiger–Siberian."
- If one set of words does not bring up the right information, try different words. For example, instead of searching for "soccer scores," try the key words "soccer" and "results."

How Do I Choose a Website?

In a library, you can check who wrote a book. You can also check who published it, and when. That can tell you how reliable a book is. When using the Internet, it's not always easy to tell who wrote or uploaded the information. So, how can you carefully choose the websites you select for research?

Look for the Endings

Anyone can post information on the Internet. That means every search you carry out will give you a range of reliable and unreliable results. Some of the information you find will have been carefully put together by experts or teachers. However, some will have been put together by unqualified people. They may not have checked the facts they mention. One easy rule to remember when looking for reliable sources is to look for websites that end in .gov (which stands for government). Also look for .edu (which stands for education), or .org (which stands for organization). Those "domain names" tell you that the site has been made by a trustworthy organization.

Linked to the Internet

Some informational books will provide ideas about where to look for more information on the Internet. These are called Internet-linked books. This means that they suggest websites you can explore to help you with your topic.

You Can Hack It!

Using **misleading** information found when researching can result in a lot of problems. Can you think of situations in which this could occur?

How Do I Check It Out?

When you find a website, work through this checklist before you use the information:

- Check if the website has a modern design. Up-to-date, well-designed sites are usually reliable.
- Check if the facts match up with what you already know. If they do not, the site may not be reliable.
- Check who wrote the information. If the website does not say who wrote the information, the author is unlikely to be an expert. Look for websites written by experts.
- Check when the information was uploaded. Reliable sites are usually updated regularly.
- Check if the information gives only one opinion. If so, it may be **biased**.
- Check if the information contains advertisements. If so, the people who created it are probably trying to sell you something.
- Check if the site can be edited by anyone. If so, it may not be trustworthy.

Chapter Three

Help! How Do I Use Information?

#KnowledgeKnow-How! Information is great, but knowing how to use it is even better! From finding facts through to knowing how to take and organize notes, understanding how to get the most out of your research will put you in the fast lane of the information highway. So let's get started.

Finding Out Fast

Some people do not have the time or patience to read through pages and pages of information. They just want to get to the facts they need to know, and fast. So, how do they do it? They skim and scan! That's right—these weird-sounding research skills can take you to the facts and stats you need super-quick.

Speedy Scanning

Scanning means flicking your eyes over a text to find specific words. People use this trick to find information such as dates, names, things, and places. If your project is about **vitamins**, you could scan over the pages of a food book, looking only for the word "vitamins."

Exhausted by endless research? Skimming and scanning could become your new best friends!

To scan information **effectively**, use these top tips:

- Take your time. If you scan too quickly, you might miss key words.
- Look only for the first few letters of a word, instead of the whole word.
- On a website source, click on the "find" option and choose key words. The computer then scans for you!

How Do I Skim?

Skimming is a way of reading a page of text to find the pieces of information that are useful, without reading every word. To skim a page, you look only at certain parts of the text. To skim:

- Read the title, the introduction or first paragraph, and the final paragraph of a long chapter. This will provide an overview of the information that chapter contains.
- Look at all of the titles, headings, and subheadings on a page. Search for any words that are in bold or italics. This will help you find any material that is important.
- Look at the illustrations, photographs, charts, and graphs. These quickly tell you what the text is about, and the images will also help you understand the subject.

You Can Hack It!

Can you think of some jobs or situations in which being able to skim and scan is useful?

Note-taking is an important part of research because it helps you to remember all of the information you have read. The best way to take notes is to read through the text once, then read it again, taking notes as you read. There are several different ways to take really great research notes.

In Your Own Words

When you rewrite what you've read in your own words, it is called paraphrasing. This helps you understand what you are reading. It also helps you focus on the points that **relate** to your project. You can check the original text to copy important spellings correctly. You can also look up words that you don't understand in the **glossary**, so you can explain them in your notes.

Learning how to take great notes can save you a lot of time when it comes to writing up your project.

How Do I Use Quotes?

If you copy something directly from a book without putting it into your own words, put quotation marks around it. This shows it is an exact quotation.

Short and Sweet

Summarizing is when you write down only the key points from a text. This could include things such as important dates, events, people, and places, for example. A summary is usually much shorter than the original text. To summarize a text, read it through once or twice. Then, write down the main points, without looking at the text again. Use bullet points instead of full paragraphs and keep the sentences short.

Make a Mark

Highlighting pages you have photocopied or printed out from the Internet is useful only if you also add your own notes and comments to them. To do this, use a highlighter pen when you first read through the text. Mark any areas of text or words that are relevant to your assignment. Then, when you read through the text for a second time, write notes in the margin. Use your own words to summarize or paraphrase the highlighted text, or to explain how it might be useful.

How Do I Get Organized?

Completed your research? Then, it's time to start organizing your notes. This will help you prepare for writing your assignment. Hopefully, you have found lots of interesting information during your research. But how can you now organize it?

So Sorted

A good way to start organizing your notes is to sort your information into different categories, or groups. First, take a few minutes to think about all the information you've gathered. Decide what the main points are. You could organize the information chronologically, which means sorting it according to when things happened. You could also group it by different ideas. For example, if you've been researching a project about lions, you might have a set of notes that you can sort into groups. This could include: "where lions live," "what lions eat," "how lions hunt," "lion cubs," and "threats to lions."

Notes? Check. Files? Check. Check you out, research rookie!

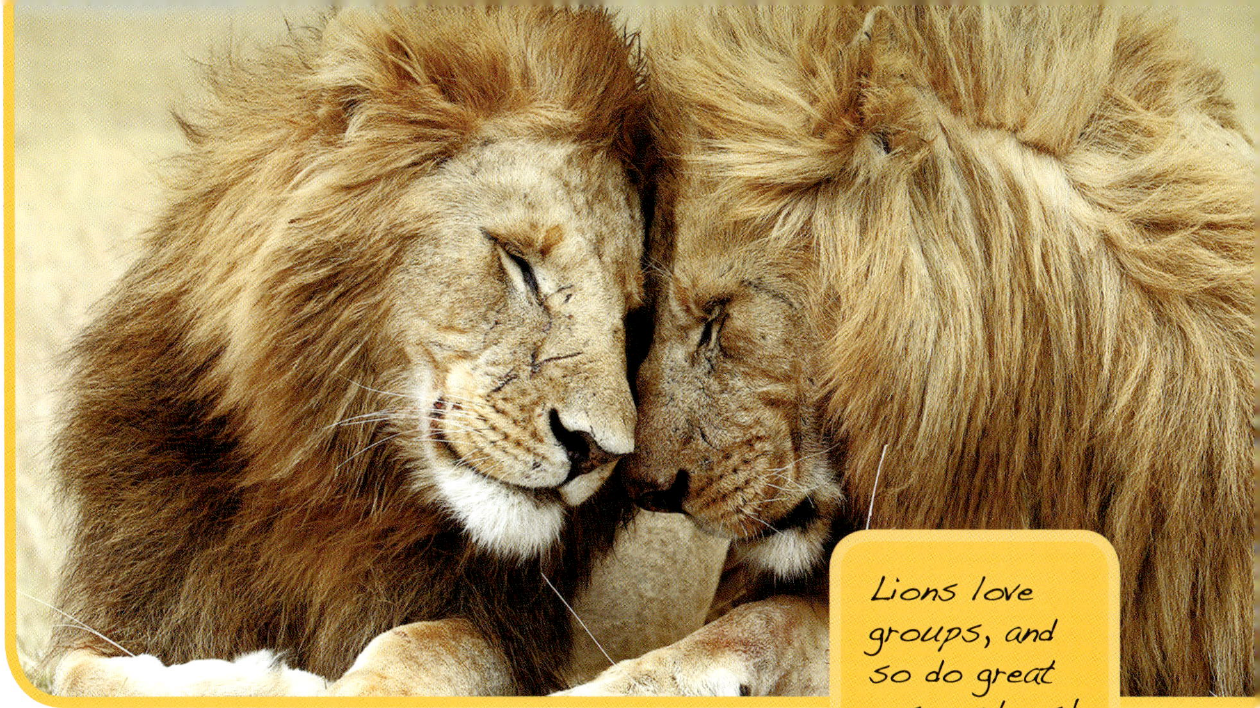

Lions love groups, and so do great researchers!

Smart Cards

Index cards are very useful because they can be easily grouped together or rearranged. Try to make note headings clear. You could even highlight them in different colors. That will make it easier to sort through your notes when it is time to write your report.

#Help!

How Do I Store Information?

You can sort your notes into lists on paper, or create a word document on your computer. You could also use note cards called index cards. Put a list of headings on a page or document, or on individual index cards. Try to stick to one idea per heading or per card. If you have a card called "What Lions Eat," you can put all the information that you've gathered about that topic on the card, or under one heading. Grouping notes in this way helps you compare the facts you have found. This helps you spot mistakes, such as two sources that say different things.

If someone lends you something, you say "thank you," right? Well, it's just the same when you borrow someone's information for research. You still need to say "thank you" for using their work. It helped you to write your project, so it is only fair that you thank the source with a note in your work. This is called "crediting."

Who Do I Need to Thank?

You can use almost anything you find in books, magazines, newspapers, or on the Internet for a school project. You just need to make sure that you give credit to the sources you used. That means noting where the information came from and who wrote it. Try to write down the source for each piece of information that you find while you're researching a project.

Never Copy!

Citing, or showing, your sources is an important way to avoid plagiarism. Plagiarism is when a writer uses someone else's words or work and claims that it is their own work. Plagiarism is a form of cheating.

You Can Hack It!

Can you think of situations in which plagiarism could get you into trouble? How would you feel if someone else copied your work and passed it off as their own?

How Do I Thank People?

People usually put a list of their sources at the end of a book or project. This list is called the bibliography. In books, the bibliography is usually written in alphabetical order by the author's last name. To write your bibliography:

- Include the title of the source, the author, and the publisher. Add the place and date of publication.
- An online source should include the title of the website and the URL address, such as:
  The Trail of Tears. http://www.pbs.org/wgbh/aia/part4/4h1567.html

Easy to Find

Another good reason to record your sources is so you can easily find them again. If you know where your notes came from, you'll have no trouble finding the book or website that the information came from.

Help! How Do I Use My Research?

#TimeToShine! You've completed all your research and organized your notes. So what's next? Now is your chance to use all that great information to create a project that will wow your teacher. Remember, you did a lot of hard work during your research—don't waste it! Take this chance to show off some of the most interesting pieces of information you have discovered.

Good preparation helps us do something well, so good research and good notes should help you produce a better piece of work.

If your notes are organized into groups or themes, all you then have to do is put them into an order that works well. Decide which parts of the research information should come first and which should follow. If your notes are grouped on index cards, just shuffle them until you have an order that you are happy with.

Shape It Up

The first step in shaping up your research project is to create an outline. An outline shows your ideas and the order in which you are going to write about them. To write your outline, first read or skim through the notes you made to remind yourself of everything you have learned. This will help you get an overview of the information and help you figure out a plan for how to use it.

Write It Up

Finally, write the information as best you can and try to add some images and quotes to make it really stand out. Make your project an example of how great research leads to great work!

Research Is for Life!

Remember, being able to research well is an amazing skill to have in all areas of your life. From shopping for sneakers through choosing which vacation to take, doing your research will help you make great choices. So now you know how to research well, use it for every decision you make!

articles written works published in print or on the Internet

atlases books of maps or charts

autobiographies people's life stories, written by themselves

biased having a prejudiced, or unfair, opinion

communicate exchange information with another person

conduct carry out

ecosystems environments, the living organisms within them, and the way in which they depend on one another

edited checked and any mistakes corrected

effectively with a good result, well

encyclopedias books that give information on many subjects or on many aspects of one subject

evidence facts or objects used to support the truth

focus concentrate on something

food chains networks of organisms that are linked because they eat or are eaten by one another

glossary an alphabetical list of words and their meanings

grammar the system and structure of language, such as sentences and paragraphs

indexes alphabetical lists of topics with the pages on which they can be found

informational providing factual information

journals newspapers or magazines that deal with a particular subject

misleading leading people away from the truth, not informing people correctly

opinion someone's views about something

original the first or earliest

overview a general look at a topic, explaining what it is about

publishers people or organizations that publish, or make public, information

quotes words that people have said or written

reference factual text

relate connect to

relevant meaningful to a topic

reliable trustworthy

reports written accounts

reptiles animals with dry scaly skin and that often lay eggs on land

research find out about something

resources sources of information

sources books or documents used to provide evidence in research

survey an investigation of people's opinions by asking them a set of questions

topic a subject or theme

vitamins substances found in some foods

Books

Greve, Meg. *Science Projects* (Hitting the Books: Skills for Reading, Writing, and Research). Rourke Educational Media, 2019.

Hord, Colleen. *Writing a Research Paper* (Hitting the Books: Skills for Reading, Writing, and Research). Rourke Educational Media, 2019.

McKenzie, Precious. *Library Skills and Internet Research* (Hitting the Books: Skills for Reading, Writing, and Research). Rourke Educational Media, 2019.

Websites

For tips for how to organize schoolwork and assignments go to:
https://kidshealth.org/PrimaryChildrens/en/teens/focused.html?WT.ac=t-ra

This site provides five ways to make online research easier:
https://kidshealth.org/PrimaryChildrens/en/teens/online-research.html?WT.ac=t-ra

For lots of details about how to write an information report visit:
www.literacyideas.com/information-report

Publisher's note to educators and parents:
All the websites featured above have been carefully reviewed to ensure that they are suitable for students. However, many websites change often, and we cannot guarantee that a site's future contents will continue to meet our high standards of educational value. Please be advised that students should be closely monitored whenever they access the Internet.

About the Authors

Sarah Eason has written many information books for children on a variety of topics. Louise Spilsbury is an award-winning author who has written hundreds of wonderful books for children. As authors, both know how important good research is.